Skateboards

Quinn M. Arnold

CREATIVE EDUCATION • CREATIVE PAPERBACKS

seedlings

Published by Creative Education and Creative Paperbacks
P.O. Box 227, Mankato, Minnesota 56002
Creative Education and Creative Paperbacks
are imprints of The Creative Company
www.thecreativecompany.us

Design by Ellen Huber; production by Mary Herrmann
Art direction by Rita Marshall
Printed in the United States of America

Photographs by Dreamstime (Chris Van Lennep), Getty Images
(Klubovy/Vetta, Nicki Pardo/The Image Bank, Karl Weatherly/
Corbis), iStockphoto (35007, 3DMAVR, Bombaert, CasarsaGuru,
HomePixel, homydesign, houdre, kokkai, Ljupco, Merkuri2,
pixdeluxe, ronen, skodonnell, THEGIFT777, Vertigo3d, Henrique
Westin, yanik88, yusufsariar), Shutterstock (Alexsey_Arz, HomeArt)

Library of Congress Cataloging-in-Publication Data
Names: Arnold, Quinn M., author.
Title: Skateboards / Quinn M. Arnold.
Series: Seedlings.
Includes index.
Summary: A kindergarten-level introduction to the self-
propelled vehicles known as skateboards, covering their
purpose, parts, and operation, and such defining features as
their decks and trucks.
Identifiers: LCCN 2018053211 / ISBN 978-1-64026-172-3
(hardcover) / ISBN 978-1-62832-735-9 (pbk) / ISBN 978-1-64000-
290-6 (eBook)

Subjects: LCSH: Skateboards—Juvenile literature.
Classification: LCC GV859.8.A77 2019 / DDC 796.22—dc23

CCSS: RI.K.1, 2, 3, 4, 5, 6, 7; RI.1.1, 2, 3, 4, 5, 6, 7;
RF.K.1, 3; RF.1.1

First Edition HC 9 8 7 6 5 4 3 2 1
First Edition PBK 9 8 7 6 5 4 3 2 1

TABLE OF CONTENTS

Time to go!

Skateboards roll along smooth paths.

They do tricks
at parks.

The board is made of wood.

Four small wheels turn under the deck.

Trucks connect the wheels to the deck.

Grip tape covers the deck.

The deck curves up at each end.

This helps the skateboarder do tricks.

A skater pushes off the ground. This makes the skateboard go.

To turn, the skater leans to the side.

One person rides on the deck at a time.

Skateboarders wear helmets. Pads may protect wrists, elbows, and knees.

One end of a deck snaps down. The skateboard lifts.

It lands and glides away.

Go, skateboard, go!

Picture a Skateboard

nose

deck

riser

truck

grip tape

tail

kingpin

wheels

deck: the part of the skateboard that a rider stands on

protect: to keep safe from injury

trucks: metal parts at each end of the board that allow riders to turn

Read More

Adamson, Thomas K. *Skateboarding Street Style*.
Minneapolis: Bellwether Media, 2016.

Donner, Erica. *Skateboarding*.
Minneapolis: Jump!, 2017.

Websites

DK Find Out!: Facts about Skateboarding
https://www.dkfindout.com/us/sports/skateboarding/
Learn more about the history and varieties of skateboarding.

YouTube: 10 Easy Beginner Skateboard Tricks
https://www.youtube.com/watch?v=hc2kh9pQq9M
Learn how to do 10 different skateboarding tricks.

Index